best of •
asia

Chef
express

Published by:
TRIDENT REFERENCE PUBLISHING
801 12th Avenue South, Suite 400
Naples, Fl 34102 USA

Tel: + 1 (239) 649-7077
www.tridentreference.com
email: sales@tridentreference.com

Best of Asia
© TRIDENT REFERENCE PUBLISHING

Publisher
Simon St. John Bailey

Editor-in-chief
Susan Knightley

Prepress
Precision Prep & Press

Includes Index
ISBN 1582797366
UPC 6 15269 97366 0

Printed in The United States

introduction

Have a look at a table full of Asian exotic dishes. It will be very difficult for you to choose among sushi subtleties, bittersweet dishes and curry fervor. That is why this book contains dishes representative of Thailand, China, Japan and India as well as some of Indonesia and Malaysia. The aim is to provide a synthetic and complete panorama of that immense continent to curious cooks.

Rather than following completely authentic formulas, we have preferred to gather creative recipes based on traditional ingredients and methods which reflect a style of cooking that we are sure will appeal to you and your guests. Go ahead then and travel to Asia taking our attractive suggestions as a starting point. And do not scare at the mentioning of uncommon products. Even though their names may be unknown to you, you can get them at supermarkets or Oriental food stores. Below you will find some references about them and so will you in "tips from the chef" at the end of the recipes.

- **Cellophane noodles** are soy noodles that become transparent when hydrated.
- **Galanga** is the root of a plant belonging to the ginger family. It has a sweet flavor and a strong aroma which reminds us of cinnamon and citrus.

- **Garam masala** is a highly scented mix of cardamom, cinnamon, nutmeg, mace and cumin.
- **Kaffir lime leaves** are the highly aromatic leaves from a citrus tree native of South-Asia.
- **Kechap manis** is a thick sweet seasoning sauce made of soy sauce, sugar and spices, used in Indonesian cooking.
- **Mirin** is amber-colored sugary wine made of rice. It is only used in cooking.
- **Nori** is a kind of seaweed. It is sold in sheets which are similar to dark green cellophane.

- **Oyster sauce** is made of oysters cooked in soy sauce and brine. It is thick, dark brown and intensely aromatic.
- **Rice vinegar** is clear, sweet and fragrant.
- **Sesame oil** is made from roasted sesame seeds and has a strong flavor.
- **Shrimp paste** is a pungent ingredient made by pounding dried salted shrimp.
- **Tamarind pulp** is made from the fruit of the tamarind or Indian date tree, which is seeded and peeled and then pressed into a dark brown pulp.
- **Thai fish sauce**, also known as **nam pla**, is the drained liquid from salted fermented anchovies. It has a pungent taste.

Difficulty scale

■□□ I Easy to do

■■□ I Requires attention

■■■ I Requires experience

seafood
and tofu soup

■ ■ ■ | Cooking time: 10 minutes - Preparation time: 10 minutes

ingredients

> **10 uncooked medium prawns, shelled and deveined, tails left intact**
> **125 g/4 oz squid, cleaned**
> **1/2 teaspoon salt**
> **1/2 teaspoon sugar**
> **1/2 teaspoon cornflour**
> **1/4 teaspoon freshly ground black pepper**
> **1/4 teaspoon sesame oil**
> **185 g/6 oz firm white fish fillets, sliced**
> **1 tablespoon vegetable oil**
> **3-5 thin slices fresh ginger**
> **300 g/9 1/2 oz tofu, sliced**
> **1 small carrot, sliced**
> **2 teaspoons chicken stock powder**
> **2-3 spring onions, cut into 2.5 cm/1 in lengths**

method

1. Cut prawns in half lengthwise. Make a single cut down the length of each squid tube or body and open out. Using a sharp knife, cut parallel lines down the length of the squid, taking care not to cut right through the flesh. Make more cuts in the opposite direction (a) to form a diamond pattern. Cut each piece into 3 or 4 pieces.
2. Place salt, sugar, cornflour, black pepper, sesame oil and 1 tablespoon water in a bowl and mix to combine. Add prawns, squid and fish (b), toss to combine and set aside to marinate for 10-15 minutes.
3. Heat vegetable oil in a wok or large saucepan, add ginger and stir-fry for 2-3 minutes or until fragrant. Stir in 3 cups/750 ml/1 1/4 pt water and bring to the boil. Add seafood mixture, tofu, carrot and chicken stock powder and cook for 5 minutes or until seafood is cooked. Remove pan from heat, sprinkle with spring onions (c) and serve immediately.

....
Serves 4

tip from the chef

Either fresh or frozen squid can be used for this dish. Freezing squid has no adverse effect on it –in fact more often than not it tenderizes it.

a

b

c

hot and sour
seafood soup

■□□ | Cooking time: 15 minutes - Preparation time: 10 minutes

method

1. Place shallots, chilies, lime leaves, ginger and stock in a saucepan and bring to the boil over a high heat. Reduce heat and simmer for 3 minutes.
2. Add fish, prawns, mussels and mushrooms and cook for 3-5 minutes or until fish and seafood are cooked, discard any mussels that do not open. Stir in lime juice and fish sauce.
3. To serve, ladle soup into bowls, scatter with coriander leaves and accompany with lime wedges.

....

Serves 6

ingredients

> 4 red or golden shallots, sliced
> 2 fresh green chilies, chopped
> 6 kaffir lime leaves
> 4 slices fresh ginger
> 8 cups/2 litres/3^1/2 pt fish, chicken or vegetable stock
> 250 g/8 oz firm fish fillets, cut into chunks
> 12 medium uncooked prawns, shelled and deveined
> 12 mussels, scrubbed and beards removed
> 125 g/4 oz oyster or straw mushrooms
> 3 tablespoons lime juice
> 2 tablespoons Thai fish sauce
> fresh coriander leaves
> lime wedges

tip from the chef

Straw mushrooms are one of the most popular mushrooms used in Asian cooking and in the West are readily available canned. Oyster mushrooms are also known as abalone mushrooms and range in color from white to grey to pale pink. Their shape is similar to that of an oyster shell and they have a delicate flavor. Oyster mushrooms should not be eaten raw as some people are allergic to them in the uncooked state.

creamy corn
and crab soup

■□□ | Cooking time: 8 minutes - Preparation time: 5 minutes

ingredients

> **440 g/14 oz canned creamed corn**
> **1³/₄ cup/440 ml/14 fl oz water**
> **185 g/6 oz crabmeat**
> **1¹/₂ teaspoons cornflour blended with 1 tablespoon water**
> **1 egg, lightly beaten**
> **1 teaspoon vinegar**
> **¹/₄ teaspoon sugar**
> **freshly ground black pepper**

method

1. Place corn and water in a saucepan and bring to the boil over a medium heat. Stir in crabmeat and cornflour mixture and bring to simmering.
2. Remove from heat, stir in egg, vinegar and sugar and season to taste with black pepper. Serve immediately.

....

Serves 4

tip from the chef

For something different make this soup using pork mince instead of the crabmeat.

chili
kumara soup

■□□ | Cooking time: 25 minutes - Preparation time: 10 minutes

method

1. Place stock, lemon grass, chilies, galanga or ginger and coriander roots in a saucepan and bring to the boil over a medium heat. Add kumara and simmer, uncovered, for 15 minutes or until soft.
2. Remove lemon grass, galanga or ginger and coriander roots and discard. Cool liquid slightly, then purée soup, in batches, in a food processor or blender.
3. Return soup to a clean saucepan and stir in 1/2 cup/125 ml/4 fl oz of the coconut cream and the fish sauce. Cook, stirring, over a medium heat for 4 minutes or until heated. Stir in two-thirds of the reserved coriander leaves.
4. To serve, ladle soup into bowls, top with a little of the remaining coconut cream and scatter with remaining coriander leaves.

....
Serves 4

ingredients

> 6 cups/1.5 litres/ 2 1/2 pt chicken stock
> 3 stalks fresh lemon grass, bruised, or 1 1/2 teaspoons dried lemon grass, soaked
> 3 fresh red chilies, halved
> 10 slices fresh or bottled galanga or fresh ginger
> 5-6 fresh coriander plants, roots washed, leaves removed and reserved
> 1 large kumara, peeled and cut into 2 cm/ 3/4 in pieces
> 3/4 cup/185 ml/6 fl oz coconut cream
> 1 tablespoon Thai fish sauce

tip from the chef

Coriander is used extensively in Thai cooking and it is one of the ingredients that gives Thai food its distinctive flavor. Fresh coriander is readily available from greengrocers and is usually sold as the whole plant.

avocado sushi

■■□ | Cooking time: 25 minutes - Preparation time: 20 minutes

ingredients

> **2 cups short grain rice**
> **3 cups water**
> **$1/3$ cup rice vinegar**
> **$1/3$ cup sugar**
> **3 teaspoons salt**
> **5 sheets nori**
> **2 teaspoons wasabi paste**
> **1 small green cucumber, peeled, seeded, cut into thin strips**
> **1 avocado, peeled, cut into thin strips**
> **60 g/2 oz sliced pickled ginger, cut into thin strips**

method

1. Combine rice and water in pan, bring to the boil, reduce heat, simmer, uncovered until water is absorbed. Cover pan, simmer 5 minutes.
2. Stir in combined vinegar, sugar and salt. Arrange nori sheets in single layer on oven tray. Toast in moderate oven 2 minutes or until crisp.
3. Cut a strip about 4 cm/$1^1/2$ in wide from the narrow end of the nori sheet. Place the large piece of nori in the center of a bamboo mat, place the extra narrow strip in the center; this helps strengthen the nori during rolling.
4. Spread about a fifth of the rice over nori. At the end furthest away from you leave a 4 cm/$1^1/2$ in edge. Make a hollow with wet fingers horizontally across the center. Spread the wasabi paste along hollow in rice. Place a combination of cucumber, avocado and ginger in hollow of rice.
5. Use bamboo mat to help roll the sushi, pressing firmly as you roll. Remove bamboo mat. Use a sharp knife to cut sushi into 4 cm/$1^1/2$ in slices.

....

Serves 4

tip from the chef

Nori, wasabi paste and pickled ginger are available from Asian food shops.

tuna
and prawn sushi

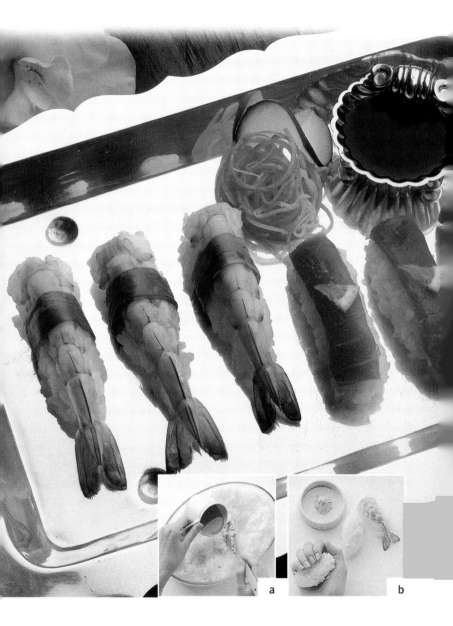

a

b

■■□ | Cooking time: 20 minutes - Preparation time: 20 minutes

method

1. To make rice, wash rice several times in cold water and set aside to drain for 30 minutes. Place rice and water in a large saucepan and bring to the boil, cover and cook, without stirring, over a low heat for 15 minutes. Remove pan from heat and set aside for 10 minutes.

2. Place mirin or sherry, vinegar, sugar and salt in a small saucepan and bring to the boil. Remove pan from heat and set aside to cool.

3. Turn rice out into a large shallow dish, pour over vinegar mixture (a) and toss gently until rice has cooled to room temperature. Take a tablespoon of rice in your hand and gently squeeze it to form a neat oval (b). Place on a serving platter and repeat with remaining rice to make 24 ovals.

4. Split prawns on the underside –taking care not to cut all the way through– and flatten them out. Mix wasabi powder with a few drops of water to make a smooth paste and dab a little on each rice oval. Top twelve rice ovals with prawns.

5. Cut tuna into twelve 2 x 4 cm/ $^3/_4$ x $1^1/_2$ in strips each 5 mm/$^1/_4$ in thick. Top remaining rice ovals with tuna strips. Wrap a strip of nori, if using, around each sushi. Serve sushi with soy sauce for dipping.

....
Makes 24

ingredients

> **12 large cooked prawns, shelled, deveined, tails left intact**
> **2 teaspoons wasabi powder**
> **125 g/4 oz extremely fresh tuna**
> **1 sheet nori, cut into strips (optional)**
> **soy sauce**

sushi rice

> **500 g/1 lb short grain rice**
> **2$^1/_2$ cups/600 ml/ 1 pt water**
> **2 tablespoons mirin or sherry**
> **4 tablespoons rice vinegar**
> **2 tablespoons sugar**
> **$^1/_2$ teaspoon salt**

tip from the chef

Strips of spring onion can be used in place of the nori if you wish. Wasabi is a very hot horseradish powder; it is available from Asian food stores.

vegetable
pilau

■□□ | Cooking time: 45 minutes - Preparation time: 10 minutes

ingredients

> 500 g/1 lb mixed
vegetables such as peas,
diced potatoes, sliced
beans, diced zucchini,
diced carrot and
cauliflower flowerets
> 2 tablespoons
vegetable oil
> 1 onion, sliced
> 1 bay leaf
> 1 cinnamon stick
> 1/2 teaspoon fennel seeds
> 1/2 teaspoon cumin seeds
> 1/2 teaspoon black
mustard seeds
> 1/2 teaspoon yellow
mustard seeds
> 1/4 teaspoon fenugreek
seeds
> 2 teaspoons finely
chopped fresh ginger
> 2 fresh red or green
chilies, finely chopped
> 2 cups/440 g/14 oz rice
> 5 cups/1.2 litres/2 pt hot
water
> 2 hard-boiled eggs, sliced
> 2 tomatoes, sliced
> 60 g/2 oz salted cashews,
roughly chopped
> 90 g/3 oz sultanas

method

1. Boil, steam or microwave vegetables until
   partially cooked. Drain and set aside.
2. Heat oil in a large saucepan, add onion,
   bay leaf, cinnamon stick, fennel, cumin,
   mustard and fenugreek seeds, ginger
   and chilies and cook over a medium heat
   for 1 minute.
3. Stir in rice and mix well to combine. Add
   mixed vegetables and cook for 2 minutes.
   Stir in hot water and transfer rice mixture
   to a casserole dish. Cover and bake at
   180°C/350°F/Gas 4 for 20-30 minutes
   or until rice is cooked.
4. Place rice mixture on a large serving
   platter. Decorate border with alternate
   slices of egg and tomato, then sprinkle with
   cashews and sultanas.

....

Serves 4

tip from the chef
*The decorative garnish is optional, but it
makes for an attractive presentation.*

a

noodle
baskets with vegetables

■ ■ □ | Cooking time: 15 minutes - Preparation time: 10 minutes

method

1. To make baskets, divide noodles into four equal portions. Use one portion of noodles to line a medium-sized metal sieve, then press another smaller metal sieve over the noodles to form a basket shape (a).
2. Heat oil in a wok over a high heat until a cube of bread dropped in browns in 50 seconds. Deep-fry noodle baskets (b) for 2 minutes or until noodles are crisp and golden. Turn basket onto absorbent kitchen paper to drain and repeat with remaining noodles to make four baskets.
3. Heat sesame oil and 1 tablespoon vegetable oil together in a clean wok over a medium heat, add spring onions, ginger and garlic and stir-fry for 2 minutes. Add carrot, red pepper and asparagus (c) and stir-fry for 3 minutes.
4. Add mushrooms, corn, soy sauce and honey and stir-fry for 2 minutes or until heated through. Spoon vegetables into noodle baskets.

ingredients

> 1 teaspoon sesame oil
> 1 tablespoon vegetable oil
> 3 spring onions, sliced
> 1 tablespoon finely grated fresh ginger
> 2 cloves garlic, crushed
> 1 carrot, sliced
> 1 red pepper, cut into thin strips
> 250 g/8 oz asparagus, cut into 5 cm/2 in lengths
> 125 g/4 oz oyster mushrooms
> 60 g/2 oz canned baby sweet corn cobs
> 1/4 cup/60 ml/2 fl oz soy sauce
> 1 tablespoon honey

noodle baskets

> 125 g/4 oz fresh thin egg noodles, cooked and drained well
> vegetable oil for deep-frying

....

Serves 4

tip from the chef

Noodle baskets can be made several hours in advance, however do not cook the vegetables and fill the baskets until immediately prior to serving.

b

c

crispy noodles with lime pickle

■□□ | Cooking time: 50 minutes - Preparation time: 15 minutes

ingredients

> 220 g/7 oz cellophane noodles
> 6 small fresh red chilies, finely sliced
> 4 red or golden shallots, finely chopped
> 30 g/1 oz fresh coriander leaves, chopped
> 30 g/1 oz fresh basil leaves, chopped
> 1 tablespoon roasted shrimp paste (optional)
> 1/4 cup/60 ml/2 fl oz peanut oil

lime pickle
> 4 limes, sliced
> 6 red or golden shallots, sliced
> 1 tablespoon salt
> 1/2 cup/125 ml/4 fl oz water
> 1/2 cup/90 g/3 oz brown sugar
> 1/4 cup/60 ml/2 fl oz vinegar
> 1 tablespoon Thai fish sauce
> 1 tablespoon black mustard seeds

method

1.To make pickle, place limes, shallots, salt and water in a saucepan and cook, stirring occasionally, over a medium heat for 10-15 minutes or until limes are tender. Stir in sugar (a), vinegar, fish sauce and mustard seeds and simmer, stirring frequently, for 30 minutes or until pickle is thick.

2.Place noodles in a bowl, pour over boiling water (b) to cover and stand for 10 minutes or until soft. Drain well. Add chilies, shallots, coriander, basil and shrimp paste (if using) to noodles and mix well.

3.Heat oil in a large frying pan over a medium heat, place small handfuls of noodle mixture in pan, shape into a rough round and flatten with a spatula (c). Cook for 3-4 minutes each side or until golden and crisp. Drain on absorbent kitchen paper and serve with pickle.

....

Serves 6

tip from the chef
When making the pickle take care not to let it catch on the bottom of the pan. The pickle can be made in advance and stored in the refrigerator or if keeping for more than 2 weeks seal in a sterilized jar.

noodle
vegetable rolls

■□□ | Cooking time: 0 minute - Preparation time: 15 minutes

method

1. Dip a rice paper round into cold water, then place on a clean tea-towel, to absorb any excess moisture.
2. To assemble, place a little of the cucumber, carrot, sprouts, noodles, mint, basil, coriander and peanuts along the center of each rice paper round leaving a 2 cm/ 3/4 in border. Place a chive (if using) across the center so that the end with the flower hangs over one edge.
3. To roll, fold up one edge of rice paper over filling to form base of roll, then roll up to enclose filling. Repeat with remaining rice paper rounds, filling and chives. Serve immediately with chili sauce for dipping.

....
Makes 12

ingredients

> 12 large rice paper rounds
> sweet chili sauce

noodle vegetable filling

> 2 cucumbers, seeded and cut into 5 cm/ 2 in strips
> 2 carrots, cut into 5 cm/2 in strips
> 60 g/2 oz bean sprouts
> 60 g/2 oz rice vermicelli noodles, cooked and drained well
> 30 g/1 oz fresh mint leaves
> 30 g/1 oz fresh basil leaves
> 15 g/1/2 oz fresh coriander leaves
> 4 tablespoons chopped roasted peanuts
> 12 garlic chives with flower (optional)

tip from the chef

Traditionally the garlic chive pops out the open end of the roll as a garnish. Oriental rice paper is made from a paste of ground rice and water which is stamped into rounds and dried. When moistened the brittle sheets become flexible. It is used to make delicacies such as these rolls. Sold in sealed packets rice paper can be purchased from Oriental food stores.

baked fish

■□□ | Cooking time: 25 minutes - Preparation time: 15 minutes

ingredients

> **2 large onions, roughly chopped**
> **1 tablespoon vegetable oil**
> **2 cloves garlic, crushed**
> **2 fresh red or green chilies, finely chopped**
> **2 teaspoons finely chopped fresh ginger**
> **1 tablespoon cumin seeds**
> **2 bay leaves**
> **4 large tomatoes, finely chopped**
> **1/2 teaspoon mango powder**
> **1/2 teaspoon ground cumin**
> **1/2 teaspoon ground coriander**
> **1/4 teaspoon ground turmeric**
> **pinch ground cloves**
> **pinch ground cinnamon**
> **pinch ground cardamom**
> **3 tablespoons cream**
> **4 firm white fish fillets**
> **1 bunch fresh basil, leaves removed and finely chopped**

method

1. Place onions in a food processor or blender and process to make a purée (a). Heat oil in a heavy-based saucepan, add garlic, chilies, ginger, cumin seeds, bay leaves and onion purée and cook over a medium heat until onions are a pinkish color. Add tomatoes (b), mango powder and spices and cook, stirring, for 3-4 minutes. Remove pan from heat and stir in cream.
2. Place fish in a baking dish, pour over sauce (c) and bake at 180°C/350°F/Gas 4 for 20 minutes or until fish flakes when tested with a fork. Just prior to serving, sprinkle with basil.

....
Serves 4

tip from the chef

Fresh herb raita is the perfect accompaniment to fish. To make raita, place 1 cup natural yogurt and 1/4 cup water in a bowl and whip until smooth. Coarsely chop 1/4 bunch coriander, 3 sprigs mint, 3 sprigs basil, 3 sprigs dill and 12 chives and add to yogurt mixture, mix to combine.

deep-fried
chili fish

■■□ | Cooking time: 15 minutes - Preparation time: 15 minutes

method

1. Make diagonal slashes along both sides of the fish.
2. Place chopped chilies, coriander roots, garlic and black peppercorns in a food processor and process to make a paste. Spread mixture over both sides of fish and marinate for 30 minutes.
3. To make sauce, place sugar, sliced chilies, shallots, vinegar and water in a saucepan and cook, stirring, over a low heat until sugar dissolves. Bring mixture to simmering and simmer, stirring occasionally, for 4 minutes or until sauce thickens.
4. Heat vegetable oil in a wok or deep-frying pan until a cube of bread dropped in browns in 50 seconds. Cook fish, one at a time, for 2 minutes each side or until crisp and flesh flakes when tested with a fork. Drain on absorbent kitchen paper. Serve with chili sauce.

ingredients

> 2 x 500 g/1 1b lean whole fish (bream, whiting or cod)
> 4 fresh red chilies, chopped
> 4 fresh coriander roots
> 3 cloves garlic, crushed
> 1 teaspoon crushed black peppercorns
> vegetable oil for deep-frying

red chili sauce

> 2/3 cup/170 g/5 1/2 oz sugar
> 8 fresh red chilies, sliced
> 4 red or golden shallots, sliced
> 1/3 cup/90 ml/3 fl oz coconut vinegar
> 1/3 cup/90 ml/3 fl oz water

....
Serves 6

tip from the chef

This dish is a stunning centerpiece for a Thai feast.

stuffed
calamari rings

■ ■ □ I Cooking time: 40 minutes - Preparation time: 20 minutes

ingredients
> **4 lettuce leaves**
> **4 large squid, cleaned, tentacles chopped**
> **4 sheets nori**
> **1/2 cup/125 ml/4 fl oz light soy sauce**
> **1/2 cup/125 ml/4 fl oz water**
> **3 tablespoons sugar**

method
1. Place lettuce leaves in a bowl, cover with boiling water, then drain.
2. Place one-quarter of the squid tentacles on a lettuce leaf, wrap up tightly (a) then enclose in a nori sheet and seal by lightly wetting the edge. Repeat with remaining tentacles, lettuce leaves and nori sheets.
3. Insert tentacle parcels in squid hoods (b) and secure ends with a wooden toothpick.
4. Place soy sauce, water and sugar in a saucepan, bring to simmering, then add squid and simmer for 30-40 minutes or until tender. Using a slotted spoon remove squid, drain and refrigerate overnight. To serve, cut into slices.

....

Makes 36 slices

tip from the chef
As a general guide, allow 250 g/8 oz of raw squid per serving when making quick-cooking dishes such as stir-fries and allow 500 g/1 lb per serving when braising or stewing. On longer cooking you will find that considerable shrinkage takes place, hence the larger quantity required.

a

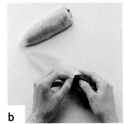

b

stir-fried
tamarind prawns

■□□ | Cooking time: 8 minutes - Preparation time: 15 minutes

method

1. Place tamarind pulp and water in a bowl and stand for 20 minutes. Strain, reserve liquid and set aside. Discard solids.
2. Heat oil in a wok or frying pan over a high heat, add lemon grass or rind and chilies and stir-fry for 1 minute. Add prawns and stir-fry for 2 minutes or until they change color.
3. Add mangoes, coriander, sugar, lime juice and tamarind liquid and stir-fry for 5 minutes or until prawns are cooked.

....

Serves 4

ingredients

> 2 tablespoons tamarind pulp
> 1/2 cup/125 ml/4 fl oz water
> 2 teaspoons vegetable oil
> 3 stalks fresh lemon grass, chopped, or 2 teaspoons finely grated lemon rind
> 2 fresh red chilies, chopped
> 500 g/1 lb medium uncooked prawns, shelled and deveined, tails left intact
> 2 green (unripe) mangoes, peeled and thinly sliced
> 3 tablespoons chopped fresh coriander leaves
> 2 tablespoons brown sugar
> 2 tablespoons lime juice

tip from the chef

Lemon grass is an aromatic herb, native of India. It is widely used in Thai and Vietnamese cooking.

shellfish
with lemon grass

■□□ | Cooking time: 10 minutes - Preparation time: 15 minutes

method

1. Place shallots, lemon grass, garlic, ginger, chilies and lime leaves in a small bowl and mix to combine.
2. Place mussels in a wok and sprinkle over half the shallot mixture. Pour in water, cover and cook over a high heat for 5 minutes.
3. Add scallops, remaining shallot mixture, lime juice, fish sauce and basil and toss to combine. Cover and cook for 4-5 minutes or until mussels and scallops are cooked. Discard any mussels that do not open.

....
Serves 4

ingredients

> 5 red or golden shallots, chopped
> 4 stalks fresh lemon grass, bruised and cut into 3 cm/1¹/4 in pieces, or 2 teaspoons dried lemon grass, soaked
> 3 cloves garlic, chopped
> 5 cm/2 in piece fresh ginger, shredded
> 3 fresh red chilies, seeded and chopped
> 8 kaffir lime leaves, torn into pieces
> 750 g/1¹/2 lb mussels, scrubbed and beards removed
> ¹/4 cup/60 ml/2 fl oz water
> 12 scallops on shells, cleaned
> 1 tablespoon lime juice
> 1 tablespoon Thai fish sauce
> 3 tablespoons fresh basil leaves

tip from the chef

Serve this dish at the table straight from the wok and don't forget to give each diner some of the delicious cooking juices.

mussels
with coconut vinegar

■ ☐ ☐ | Cooking time: 10 minutes - Preparation time: 10 minutes

method

1. Place mussels, coriander, lemon grass, ginger and water in a wok over a high heat. Cover and cook for 5 minutes or until mussels open. Discard any mussels that do not open. Remove mussels from wok, discard coriander, lemon grass and ginger. Strain cooking liquid and reserve.

2. Heat oil in a wok over a medium heat, add onion and chilies and stir-fry for 3 minutes or until onion is soft. Add mussels, reserved cooking liquid and coconut vinegar and stir-fry for 2 minutes or until mussels are heated. Scatter with coriander leaves and serve.

....
Serves 4

ingredients

> 1.5 kg/3 lb mussels, scrubbed and beards removed
> 6 whole coriander plants, washed and roughly chopped
> 3 stalks fresh lemon grass, bruised, or 1 1/2 teaspoons dried lemon grass, soaked
> 5 cm/2 in piece fresh ginger, shredded
> 1/2 cup/125 ml/4 fl oz water
> 1 tablespoon vegetable oil
> 1 red onion, halved and sliced
> 2 fresh red chilies, sliced
> 2 tablespoons coconut vinegar
> fresh coriander leaves

tip from the chef

This dish is delicious served with boiled egg noodles and topped with coriander leaves and wok juices.
Coconut vinegar is made from the sap of the coconut palm. It is available from Oriental food shops. If unavailable any mild vinegar can be used instead.

chicken
in oyster sauce

■□□ | Cooking time: 10 minutes - Preparation time: 10 minutes

ingredients
> **2 1/2 tablespoons vegetable oil**
> **500 g/1 lb chicken pieces, chopped into bite-sized pieces**
> **4 fresh green chilies, cut into 1 cm/1/2 in pieces**
> **3 thin slices fresh ginger**
> **1/3 cup/90 ml/3 fl oz oyster sauce**
> **1 teaspoon dark soy sauce**
> **1/2 teaspoon sugar**
> **1/2 teaspoon salt**
> **2 cloves garlic, sliced**
> **2 spring onions, sliced diagonally**
> **2 tablespoons chopped fresh coriander**

method
1. Heat oil in a wok or frying pan over a high heat. Add chicken, chilies and ginger and stir-fry for 3-4 minutes or until chicken is golden.
2. Stir in oyster sauce, soy sauce, sugar, salt and garlic and stir-fry for 3-4 minutes longer or until chicken is cooked. Sprinkle with spring onions and coriander and serve immediately.

....
Serves 4

tip from the chef
When handling fresh chilies do not put your hands near your eyes or allow them to touch your lips. To avoid discomfort and burning, wear rubber gloves. Freshly minced chili is available in jars from supermarkets.

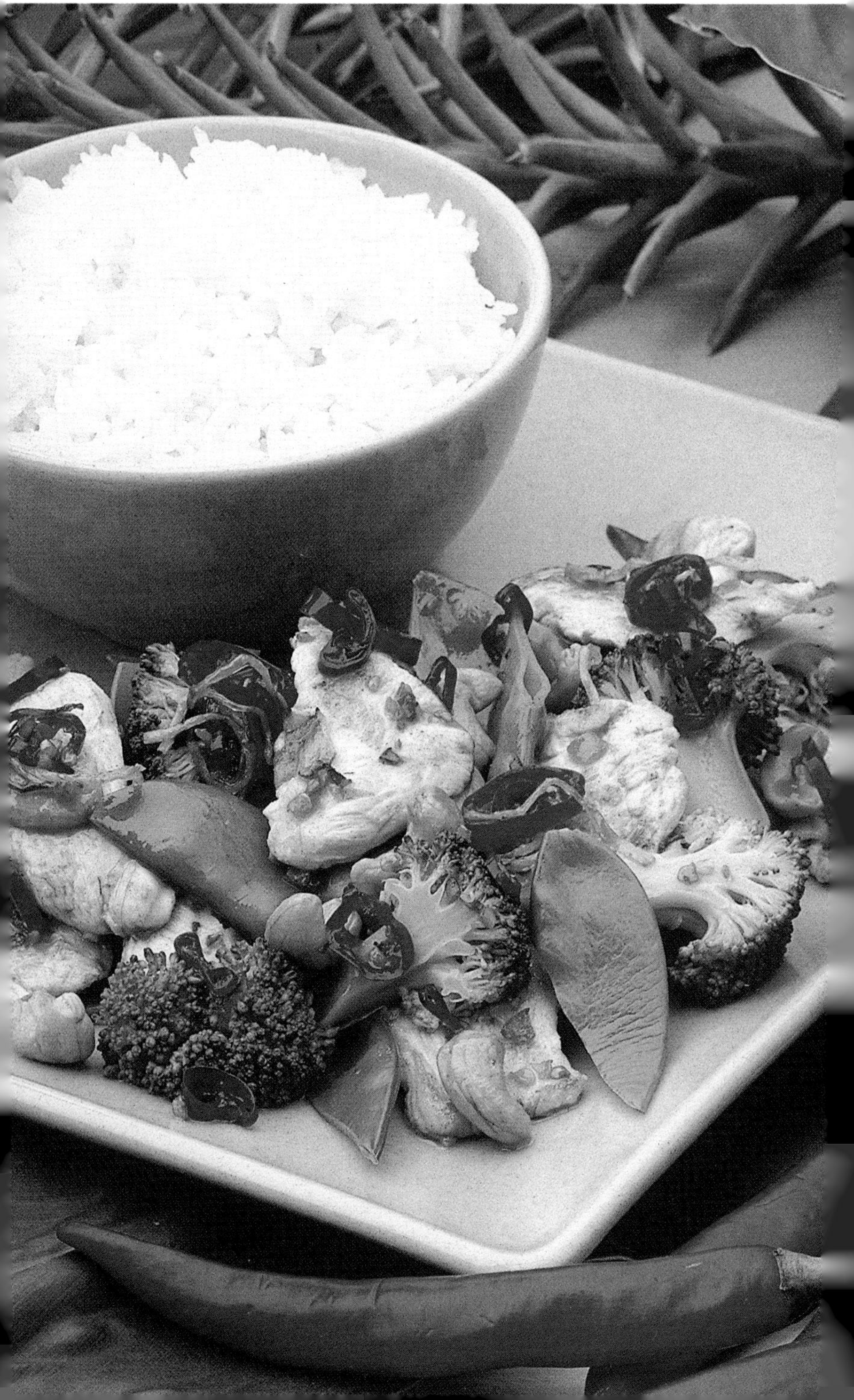

chicken
with chili jam

■□□ | Cooking time: 12 minutes - Preparation time: 10 minutes

method

1. To make jam, heat oil in a wok over a medium heat, add chilies, ginger and shrimp paste and stir-fry for 1 minute or until golden. Stir in sugar, water and lime juice and cook, stirring, for 3 minutes or until mixture is thick. Remove jam from wok and set aside.
2. Heat oil in a clean wok over a high heat for 1 minute, add chicken and shallots and stir-fry for 3 minutes or until lightly browned.
3. Add broccoli, snow peas, cashews and soy sauce and stir-fry for 3 minutes longer or until vegetables change color and are cooked.
4. To serve, place chicken on serving plate and top with chili jam.

Serves 4

ingredients

> 2 teaspoons vegetable oil
> 3 boneless chicken breast fillets, cut into thin strips
> 4 red or golden shallots, chopped
> 185 g/6 oz broccoli, chopped
> 125 g/4 oz snow peas, halved
> 60 g/2 oz unsalted roasted cashews
> 2 tablespoons soy sauce

chili jam

> 2 teaspoons vegetable oil
> 4 fresh red chilies, sliced
> 1 tablespoon shredded fresh ginger
> 1 teaspoon shrimp paste
> 1/3 cup/90 g/3 oz sugar
> 1/3 cup/90 ml/3 fl oz water
> 2 tablespoons lime juice

tip from the chef

Serve this tasty chicken dish with steamed jasmine rice. If you prefer, the chili jam can be served separately so that each diner can season their serving according to individual taste.

charcoal-grilled chicken

■□□ | Cooking time: 30 minutes - Preparation time: 15 minutes

ingredients
> 1 kg/2 lb chicken pieces
> 4 fresh red chilies, chopped
> 4 cloves garlic, chopped
> 3 fresh coriander roots, chopped
> 2 stalks fresh lemon grass, chopped, or 1 teaspoon dried lemon grass, soaked
> 3 tablespoons lime juice
> 2 tablespoons soy sauce
> 1 cup/250 ml/8 fl oz coconut cream
> sweet chili sauce

method
1. Place chicken in a ceramic or glass dish and set aside.
2. Place chilies, garlic, coriander roots, lemon grass, lime juice and soy sauce in a food processor and process to make paste. Mix paste with coconut cream and pour over chicken. Marinate for 1 hour.
3. Drain chicken and reserve marinade. Cook chicken over a slow charcoal or gas barbecue or under a preheated low grill, brushing frequently with reserved marinade, for 25-30 minutes or until chicken is tender. Serve with chili sauce.

....
Serves 6

tip from the chef
Fresh lemon grass is available from Oriental food shops and some supermarkets and greengrocers. It is also available dried; if using dried lemon grass soak it in hot water for 20 minutes or until soft before using.

savory pancakes

a

■□□ | Cooking time: 15 minutes - Preparation time: 10 minutes

method

1. To make pancakes, whisk all ingredients (a) until smooth. Heat a lightly greased wok over a high heat, pour 2 tablespoons batter and swirl wok so batter covers base thinly and evenly. Cook for 1-2 minutes or until bubbles form on the surface, turn (b) and cook until golden. Remove from wok and keep warm. Repeat with remaining batter.
2. To make filling, soak mushrooms in boiling water for 10 minutes or until tender. Drain, remove stalks and dice mushrooms. Heat oil in a wok over a medium heat, stir-fry onion for 2-3 minutes. Add mince and stir-fry for 2-3 minutes or until it changes color. Stir in carrot, mushrooms, soy sauce, salt, sesame oil, sugar and black pepper and cook for 4-5 minutes longer. Add potato (c) and coriander, mix. Remove from heat, cool.
3. Divide filling between pancakes, fold in sides and roll up. Serve hot or warm.

....
Makes 8

ingredients

pancakes

> 1 cup/125 g/4 oz flour
> 1/4 teaspoon salt
> pinch sugar
> 1 cup/250 ml/8 fl oz water
> 1 egg
> 1 teaspoon vegetable oil

meat and vegetable filling

> 3 dried Chinese mushrooms, diced
> 1 tablespoon vegetable oil
> 1 small onion, diced
> 125 g/4 oz mince of your choice
> 1 small carrot, diced
> 1 teaspoon light soy sauce
> 1/2 teaspoon salt
> 1/2 teaspoon sesame oil
> 1/2 teaspoon sugar
> pinch black pepper
> 2 large potatoes, cooked and mashed
> 2 tablespoons chopped fresh coriander

b   c

tip from the chef

This dish can be made ahead of time and reheated in the microwave on High (100%) for 2 minutes.

bean sprouts and pork stir-fry

■□□ | Cooking time: 8 minutes - Preparation time: 10 minutes

ingredients

> **4 dried Chinese mushrooms**
> **1 teaspoon oyster sauce**
> **sugar**
> **1 teaspoon soy sauce**
> **1/4 teaspoon salt**
> **1/4 teaspoon sesame oil**
> **pinch sugar**
> **pinch freshly ground black pepper**
> **185 g/6 oz lean pork, cut into thin strips**
> **2 tablespoons vegetable oil**
> **2.5 cm/1 in piece fresh ginger, cut into thin strips**
> **250 g/8 oz bean sprouts**
> **2 spring onions, cut into 5 cm/2 in strips**
> **1/2 red pepper, cut into thin strips**
> **2 cloves garlic, sliced**
> **1/2 teaspoon cornflour blended with 1 1/2 tablespoons water and 1/4 teaspoon sesame oil**

method

1. Place mushrooms in a bowl, cover with boiling water and soak for 10 minutes or until mushrooms are tender. Drain, remove stalks and cut mushrooms into strips. Place mushrooms in a small bowl, add oyster sauce and 1/4 teaspoon sugar, toss to coat and set aside.

2. Place soy sauce, salt, sesame oil, sugar and black pepper in a bowl and mix to combine. Add pork, toss to combine and marinate for 10-15 minutes.

3. Heat 1 tablespoon vegetable oil in a wok or frying pan over a medium heat, add pork mixture, mushrooms and ginger and stir-fry for 2-3 minutes or until pork changes color. Remove pork mixture from pan and set aside.

4. Heat remaining vegetable oil in pan over a medium heat, add bean sprouts, spring onions, red pepper and garlic and stir-fry for 1 minute. Return pork mixture to pan and stir in cornflour mixture. Cook, stirring, for 1 minute or until mixture thickens slightly and is heated through.

....
Serves 4

tip from the chef

Chinese mushrooms are pretty expensive, but you will need only a few to give this dish a special touch.

spicy mince stir-fry

■ □ □ | Cooking time: 8 minutes - Preparation time: 10 minutes

method

1. Heat oil in a wok or frying pan over a high heat, add onion and chilies and stir-fry for 2-3 minutes or until fragrant.
2. Add garlic, beef, mushrooms, peas, light soy sauce, Worcestershire sauce, cornflour mixture, kechap manis, sugar, salt and black pepper and stir-fry for 5 minutes or until mixture is almost dry.
3. Remove pan from heat, stir in coriander and serve immediately.

....

Serves 4

ingredients

> 1½ tablespoons vegetable oil
> 1 onion, chopped
> 2 fresh red chilies, chopped
> 1 clove garlic, chopped
> 500 g/1 lb lean beef mince
> 2 mushrooms, chopped
> 125 g/4 oz fresh or frozen peas
> 1½ tablespoons soy sauce
> 1½ tablespoons Worcestershire sauce
> 1 teaspoon cornflour blended with 1 tablespoon water
> ½ teaspoon kechap manis
> 1 teaspoon sugar
> ¾ teaspoon salt
> ¼ teaspoon freshly ground black pepper
> 1 tablespoon chopped fresh coriander

tip from the chef

This mixture is delicious served in lettuce cups. Spoon the mixture into the lettuce leaves, roll up and eat.

If kechap manis is unavailable a mixture of soy sauce and golden syrup can be used in its place.

sweet
and sour pork

■□□ | Cooking time: 15 minutes - Preparation time: 15 minutes

ingredients
> 1/2 teaspoon salt
> 1/2 teaspoon sugar
> 1/4 teaspoon freshly ground pepper
> 3/4 teaspoon light soy sauce
> 1 egg yolk
> 375 g/12 oz diced lean pork
> cornflour
> oil for deep-frying

sweet and sour sauce
> 1 tablespoon vegetable oil
> 1/2 cup/125 ml/4 fl oz water
> 2 teaspoons white vinegar
> 1/2 teaspoon sesame oil
> 1/4 teaspoon salt
> 3 tablespoons sugar
> 2 1/2 tablespoons tomato sauce
> 2 teaspoons chili sauce
> 2 teaspoons Worcestershire sauce
> 1 tablespoon cornflour blended with 2 1/2 tablespoons water
> 1 onion, cut into eighths and separated
> 1 tomato, cut into eighths
> 1 cucumber, cut into chunks
> 125 g/4 oz pineapple pieces
> 1/2 red pepper, seeded and finely chopped

method
1. Combine salt, sugar, pepper, soy sauce and egg yolk. Add pork and toss to coat. Drain pork, toss in cornflour (a). Heat oil in a wok, cook pork in batches (b) for 5 minutes or until golden. Remove and drain on absorbent kitchen paper. Keep warm.
2. To make sauce, heat oil in a wok, stir in water, vinegar, sesame oil, seasonings and sauces. Bring to simmering, stirring. Add cornflour mixture and cook, stirring, for 3-4 minutes or until sauce boils and thickens. Add remaining ingredients (c) and cook, stirring, for 1 minute. Add pork and cook for 1-2 minutes longer or until heated through.

....
Serves 4

tip from the chef
This famous dish is delicious served with boiled rice and steamed Chinese cabbage.

a b

c

barbecued
pork spare ribs

■□□ | Cooking time: 15 minutes - Preparation time: 10 minutes

method

1. Place garlic, ginger, sugar, cumin and soy sauce in a glass or ceramic bowl and mix to combine. Add spare ribs, turn to coat and marinate for 1 hour.
2. Drain ribs and reserve marinade. Cook ribs over a preheated hot barbecue or under a hot grill, basting frequently with marinade, for 15 minutes or until pork is cooked through and skin crackles.

....
Serves 6

ingredients

> **4 cloves garlic, chopped**
> **2 tablespoons finely grated fresh ginger**
> **2 tablespoons sugar**
> **2 teaspoons ground cumin**
> **1/2 cup dark soy sauce**
> **1 kg/2 lb pork spare ribs**

tip from the chef

For an informal meal, serve these tasty spare ribs with a salad of Asian greens and herbs and bowls of steamed jasmine rice.

lamb
kofta in cream sauce

■□□ | Cooking time: 50 minutes - Preparation time: 15 minutes

ingredients

lamb kofta
> 1 kg/2 lb lamb mince
> 2 tablespoons cream
> 2 teaspoons finely chopped fresh ginger
> 2 fresh chilies, finely chopped
> 3 cloves garlic, finely chopped
> 1 teaspoon mango powder
> 1 1/2 teaspoons each ground coriander, cumin and garam masala

cream sauce
> 1 tablespoon vegetable oil
> 2 bay leaves
> 2 teaspoons finely chopped fresh ginger
> 2 fresh chilies, finely chopped
> 3 cloves garlic, finely chopped
> 1 teaspoon each cumin seeds, mango powder, ground coriander, turmeric and garam masala
> 300 ml/9 1/2 fl oz cream
> 1 bunch fresh coriander, leaves chopped

method

1. To make kofta, combine all ingredients. Using wet hands, mold mixture into oval rissoles (a) and place in a steamer. Place steamer over a saucepan of boiling water (b), cover and steam for 15-20 minutes or until kofta is just cooked. Remove kofta from steamer and place in a shallow ovenproof dish. Set aside.

2. To make sauce, heat oil in a saucepan over a low heat, add spices and cook for 2 minutes. Stir in cream and cook, stirring, for 5-7 minutes. Remove from heat and stir in coriander. Spoon over kofta (c), cover and bake at 150°C/300°F/Gas 2 for 20 minutes.

....
Serves 6

tip from the chef
If you wish to offer spicy rice as a side dish for this tasty meatballs, wrap 1/4 teaspoon each black peppercorns, black mustard seeds and cumin seeds, 2 dried red chilies, 1 cinnamon stick, 2 cardamom pods, 2 teaspoons chopped fresh ginger and 2 bay leaves in a piece of muslin, tie securely. Place 5 cups/1.2 litres/2 pt water in a saucepan and bring to the boil. Stir in 2 cups/440 g/ 14 oz rice, 1 teaspoon lemon juice and spice bag and bring back to the boil, then reduce heat to low, cover and simmer for 12-15 minutes or until rice is cooked.

a

b

c

mogul lamb

Cooking time: 135 minutes - Preparation time: 15 minutes

method

1. Melt butter in a large saucepan, add tomatoes, chilies, ginger and garlic and cook over a medium heat, stirring frequently, for 15 minutes or until tomatoes are soft and pulpy.
2. Place black pepper, cardamom, cloves, fennel, cinnamon, fenugreek and water in a bowl and mix to combine. Stir spice mixture into tomato mixture, then add coriander, mint, basil and dill. Remove sauce from heat.
3. Place lamb in a glass or ceramic baking dish, pour over sauce, cover and marinate in the refrigerator for 15-20 hours.
4. Remove cover from baking dish and bake lamb at 180°C/350°F/Gas 4 for 2 hours or until cooked to your liking.

Serves 6

ingredients

> 15 g/ 1/2 oz butter
> 750 g/1 1/2 lb ripe tomatoes, finely chopped
> 2-3 fresh red or green chilies, finely chopped
> 2 teaspoons finely chopped fresh ginger
> 4 cloves garlic, finely chopped
> 1 teaspoon freshly ground black pepper
> 1/2 teaspoon each ground cardamom, cloves, fennel, cinnamon and fenugreek
> 1/2 cup/125 ml/4 fl oz water
> 2 bunches fresh coriander, leaves chopped
> 1/2 bunch fresh mint, leaves chopped
> 1/4 bunch fresh basil, leaves chopped
> 1/4 bunch fresh dill, chopped
> 1 x 1.5 kg/3 lb leg of lamb

tip from the chef

A quicker version of this dish uses 1 kg/2 lb diced lamb, rather than a leg. Heat butter in a saucepan with chilies, ginger and garlic. Add diced lamb and cook over a low heat for 30-40 minutes. Add black pepper, cardamom, cloves, fennel, cinnamon and fenugreek and cook for 10 minutes. Stir in tomatoes and cook for 20-30 minutes or until lamb is tender. Add coriander, basil, mint and dill and cook for 5 minutes longer.

rose-flavored
dessert

■□□ | Cooking time: 10 minutes - Preparation time: 10 minutes

ingredients

gulabs
> 1 cup/75 g/2¹/₂ oz skim milk powder
> ¹/₃ cup/45 g/1¹/₂ oz self-raising flour
> 15 g/ ¹/₂ oz ghee (clarified butter)
> 100 ml/3¹/₂ fl oz cream
> vegetable oil for deep-frying

syrup
> 7 cups/1.6 litres/ 3 pt water
> 3 cups/750 g/1¹/₂ lb sugar
> ¹/₂ teaspoon ground cardamom
> 2 teaspoons rosewater

method

1. To make syrup, place water, sugar, cardamom and rosewater in a large saucepan, cover and bring to a slow boil over a low heat.

2. To make gulabs, place milk powder, flour and ghee in a food processor and process to combine. With machine running, add enough cream to form a moist dough. Roll dough into 2 cm/³/₄ in balls.

3. Heat oil in a wok until a ball dropped in sizzles slowly. Reduce heat, add remaining gulabs and cook, stirring gently, until gulabs rise to the surface. Using a slotted spoon, turn them constantly until dark golden brown.

4. Increase heat under syrup. Remove gulabs from oil and add to boiling syrup. Reduce heat and cook for 2-3 minutes or until gulabs expand and become soft. Remove pan from heat. Serve gulabs warm or at room temperature with ice cream or whipped cream if desired.

....

Makes about 20

tip from the chef

When cooking gulabs in the oil they must be rolled constantly and cooked quickly to prevent them from drying out and cracking. When cooking gulabs in the syrup take care not to overcook or they will become too soft and will break.

fruit salad
with almond jelly

■□□ | Cooking time: 8 minutes - Preparation time: 10 minutes

method

1. Place agar-agar powder, sugar and a little water in a bowl and mix to dissolve. Place remaining water in a saucepan and bring to the boil over a medium heat. Lower heat, stir in agar-agar mixture and cook, stirring constantly, for 5 minutes.

2. Remove pan from heat, stir in almond essence and evaporated milk and mix well to combine. Pour mixture into a shallow 20 cm/8 in square cake tin and refrigerate until set.

3. To serve, place fruit salad and lychees with juice in a large bowl. Cut jelly into bite-sized cubes and add to fruit mixture. Chill until ready to serve.

ingredients

> 2¹/2 teaspoons agar-agar powder
> ¹/4 cup/60 g/2 oz caster sugar
> 2 cups/500 ml/16 fl oz water
> ¹/2 teaspoon almond essence
> 75 ml/2¹/2 fl oz evaporated milk
> 440 g/14 oz canned fruit salad
> 440 g/14 oz canned lychees

....
Serves 10-12

tip from the chef

Agar-agar is an extract of seaweed and is used by vegetarians instead of gelatin.

semolina
cream

■□□ | Cooking time: 40 minutes - Preparation time: 15 minutes

ingredients

> **30 g/1 oz ghee (clarified butter)**
> **2 cups/400 g/12^1/$_2$ oz fine semolina**
> **1 tablespoon sultanas**
> **1 tablespoon unsalted pistachios**
> **^{1}/$_2$ cup/125 ml/4 fl oz milk**

syrup

> **2 cups/500 ml/16 fl oz water**
> **2 cups/500 g/1 lb sugar**
> **1 tablespoon cardamom seeds**
> **pinch yellow food-coloring powder**

method

1. To make syrup, place water, sugar, cardamom seeds and food-coloring powder in a large saucepan and bring to the boil over a medium heat. Strain syrup, set aside and keep warm.

2. Melt ghee in heavy-based saucepan, stir in semolina and cook over a low heat, stirring constantly, for 20-30 minutes or until semolina changes color slightly. Take care not to burn semolina

3. Stir sultanas and pistachios into semolina mixture and cook for 3 minutes. Stir in syrup and milk and cook over a low heat, stirring constantly, for 3 minutes or until mixture thickens. Allow to cool and pour into serving glasses.

....

Serves 6

tip from the chef

Semolina cream is delicious served with whipped cream or ice cream.

index